Original title:
The Watchmaker's Journey

Copyright © 2025 Creative Arts Management OÜ
All rights reserved.

Author: Alec Donovan
ISBN HARDBACK: 978-1-80586-213-0
ISBN PAPERBACK: 978-1-80586-685-5

Crafting Time's Legacy

In a shop filled with springs and gears,
A watchmaker dances, sipping on beers.
He fixes the clocks that tick and tock,
While humming along to a ticking rock.

With a wink and a grin, he juggles the cogs,
His cat naps gently, lost in the blogs.
As pendulums swing, he cracks a few jokes,
Turning time-wmsters into laughing folks.

Beyond the Gearbox

Deep in the workshop, wild ideas spark,
Where a rubber chicken beats the clock's dark.
He tunes up a watch with a rubber band,
And out comes a melody, perfectly planned.

With gears that giggle and springs that twirl,
He dreams of a dance with a ticking swirl.
The clocks have personalities, quite the show!
As time ticks by, their antics grow.

Memories in Motion

He plucks at the dials, what a sight to see!
Each tick recalls a funny memory.
A llama in a top hat, a fish in a tie,
Every second's a tale, oh me, oh my!

The hands spin faster, the stories unfold,
With laughter and joy, they never grow old.
He repairs with a chuckle, a wink, and a shove,
This journey spins brightly, a dance filled with love.

The Clockwork Heart

In a clockwork chest where the laughter resides,
He winds up the jokes and the silliness hides.
With gears that waddle and springs that play,
Every tick and tock brightens the day.

A heart made of metal, a soul full of cheer,
The watchmaker chuckles, "Time's loved this year!"
With laughter as oil, each clock finds its beat,
In this whimsical world, life's perfectly sweet!

Temporal Footprints

In a world where clocks do squeak,
I'd race the tick, so fast, so sleek.
The hour hand, it plays a game,
With minutes lost, it's quite the shame.

With every tock, my shoes would fly,
Chasing seconds, oh my, oh my!
But all's a blur, I run amiss,
Step on a gear, and off I hiss!

Each moment counts, or so they say,
But my feet just want to play.
I'll flip a switch, and what's the cost?
Find me laughing, time's now lost!

So as I zip through space and rhyme,
I dance along, defying time.
With every tick, a grin unwinds,
In this mad race, joy I find.

A Journey Through Time's Labyrinth

In the maze where seconds dance,
I stumbled 'round, a funny stance.
Forks in the road? I just can't see,
Whispering clocks say, "Follow me!"

Each corner turned, I face surprise,
A pocket watch with silly eyes.
It winks, it blinks, with laughter loud—
"Come find your way, you time-bound crowd!"

A grandfather clock, all dressed in spats,
Cracks a pun as I tip my hats.
"It's all in good fun, don't you fret,
Just learn to laugh, then don't forget!"

So onward through the wibbly wobbly,
Past hourglasses, all so jolly.
With every twist, I meet my peers,
A timeless frolic, with grins and cheers!

Ticking Through Time

Tick-tock, what's that you say?
I'll race you to the end of day!
But oh dear clock, you skipped my cue,
Now I'm late for tea with you!

I'd hand you gears and you'd lend me time,
We'd sip on seconds with lemon lime.
A cuckoo bird might join the fun,
Laughing loud, 'til day is done.

When sundials frown, I'll wear a grin,
Finding joy in every spin.
Each tick could be a brand new chance,
To dance with time in witty dance.

So here we are, together now,
Ticking through fun, and oh, just how!
With every beat, my heart does race,
In this ticking world, there's endless space!

Gears of Destiny

In a workshop full of clunky bits,
I mix my dreams with goofy scripts.
A turn of gears, a twist of fate,
Oh, what a sight when clocks misstate!

I'd build a device to fly and spin,
But then it lands where laughs begin.
A whirlybird with springs and sass,
Takes me back to the first class pass!

"Time is stretchy," so says my gear,
It giggles soft, while I just cheer.
With every turn, I find delight,
In the wobbly dance, from day to night.

So here's to whimsy, let's get set,
In this life of tick, I have no regret.
With laughter loud and gears that shine,
We'll spin through fate, oh how divine!

Craft Beyond the Clock

In a shop where gears jiggle and twirl,
Hands spin tales in a mechanical whirl.
A pendulum swings with a hiccup and nod,
Tickling the seconds, oh my, how odd!

With springs that laugh and cogs that dance,
A rhythm of humor in every glance.
Each timepiece chuckles, a giggle or two,
As they chime their tales, just for you!

A pocket watch winks, a benevolent tease,
While cuckoos pop out with cheeky decrees.
They serve up the minutes with whimsy and flair,
In this clockwork circus, no time for despair!

So come join the fun, let the laughter unwind,
With tick-tock companions of the quirkiest kind.
In a world where each second's a joke on the shelf,
You're bound to smile—just don't tell the elf!

Seconds in Flight

Once a second, it soared through the sky,
Bumping into minutes as they floated by.
It laughed at the hours, so serious and spry,
"Hey there, my friends, give flying a try!"

A rogue little tick that was up to some fun,
Gave a wink to the clock and then suddenly spun.
It dove and it darted, a mischievous sprite,
Chasing after shadows till the moon felt polite.

With the hands in a tangle, they spun and they raced,
The time on their faces a colorful haste.
Sundials were grinning, the hourglass swayed,
As laughter erupted in time's grand parade!

So, next time you glance at the face on the wall,
Remember those seconds that dance and that sprawl.
In the realm of the clocks, oh, what joyous delight,
Let the tick-tock humor make your day bright!

An Odyssey of Springs

A spring flew off, what a sight,
It bounced and twirled, pure delight.
I chased it down, it made me giggle,
Oh, the places that it did wiggle!

Cogs danced in a merry parade,
Tick tocks played, a wild charade.
I swapped a gear for a slice of pie,
The clock groaned loud with a sigh!

With every tick, the mischief grew,
Time wobbled like a pig on cue.
But watch it slip, the hourglass laughed,
In this wild tale, we're quite daft!

So here we stand, with springs galore,
Crafting time as legends soar.
With every tick, a funny spree,
In this odd world, just you and me!

Within the Clock's Embrace

A ticklish gear, an unwound tale,
Spinning stories weaves a trail.
In cogs and springs, we find such glee,
Dancing shadows, wild and free.

A pendulum swings, a jesting fool,
Tickling time, breaking all the rules.
Tick tock, tick tock, a race to beat,
As seconds giggle beneath our feet.

I hear a watch whisper, 'What's the rush?'
With every second, we laugh and hush.
So let's unwind with a quirky tune,
And share our dreams with a silver spoon!

For in this clock's embrace so tight,
We find the giggle, the dance, the light.
So pull a lever, let mischief thrive,
In this funny clock, we come alive!

Sketches of Time

In the gallery of gears, I sketch away,
Drawing ticks that love to play.
A canvas brushed with seconds bold,
Stories of time, both shy and sold.

With a wink, the hour hand strayed,
Painting moments, never afraid.
Each tick a stroke, each tock a flair,
Art in motion fills the air!

A clockwork muse with an elbow nudge,
Tickles my fancy, refuses to budge.
With laughter echoes, we twist and bend,
Creating a ruckus, on time we depend!

So grab your brush, let's make it shine,
Sketches of laughter in this realm divine.
Together we'll tick, together we'll rhyme,
In this funny world where we conquer time!

Echoes of a Ticking Heart

A heart in gears, beats loud and clear,
Ticking softly, whisking away fear.
In the echoes, laughter swoops,
As time pirouettes with joyous hoops.

With every chime, a giggle's born,
Not a frown in sight, just chaos sworn.
The heart does laugh, oh what a tease,
In this merry dance, we find such ease!

Spring-loaded joy, twirling away,
Shifting seconds, come what may.
A clock that giggles, a heart in play,
Time crafts magic, every day!

So let's embrace the ticking show,
With every pulse, let laughter flow.
In this quirky time, we find our part,
Echoes ringing in a ticking heart!

An Heirloom in Cogs

In a shop full of gears, laughter spills,
A clock that ticks loud has some odd frills.
With springs that dance and pendulums sway,
Time giggles softly, won't slip away.

A grandfather clock, with a mischievous grin,
Keeps time with style, laughter within.
Its face says 'wise,' but its hands are a tease,
As it zones out, catching a catnap with ease.

Tiny tools scattered, like toys in the sand,
He measures each tick with a delicate hand.
Yet every mistake brings a chuckle, a sigh,
For in fixing time, the quirks multiply.

So here's to the craftsman with a heart full of cheer,
In a world of gidgets, he holds time near.
A flip of a switch, a turn of a dial,
Turns minutes to memories, with a wink and a smile.

Between Ticks and Tocks

In a world of ticks, where chaos reigns,
Time refuses to march, instead it complains.
A clock that runs backward, what a wild sight,
Said it saw 'tomorrow' take off in flight.

Cogs and levers all lined up in a row,
Chasing a second just like a show.
With each little click, the laughter erupts,
Making sense of nonsense as time interrupts.

With a twist and a twirl, the hands start to dance,
They tango with seconds, not leaving to chance.
Each tock brings a giggle, each tick brings a smile,
In the playful rhythm, let's bask for a while.

So here's to the chaos of chronometers grand,
Where time holds a party with no end planned.
In a world where ticks tumble, and tocks are so keen,
Life's just a jest, in a clockwork machine.

Shaping the Infinite

In a workshop of wonders, gears fly about,
Shaping odd moments that make us all shout.
With laughter like thunder, the cogs start to quake,
As the hands twist and turn, get ready, for fate!

A compass that spins like a whirling dervish,
Directions are lost, but dreams always flourish.
With every mistake, a new path's revealed,
In the funny math of time that's concealed.

With hammers and jokes, the clockmaker toils,
Creating a rhythm that beautifully spoils.
Tickling time's fancy with whims of delight,
Crafting the universe, with giggles in sight.

So come join the fun, in this wild little place,
Where time is a jester, and laughter's an ace.
In shaping the endless, let mischief ensue,
As the world spins in circles, just for me and you.

Time's Artisan's Muse

In the tangle of springs, creativity flows,
Ticking away at the troubles that pose.
With every little gears' hum and sigh,
Time paints a story that flutters and flies.

A clock with a wink, and a sly little laugh,
Hums tunes of the cosmos, sketches a path.
While hours frolic and seconds ensnare,
In the dance of the artisans, chaos is rare.

With wrenches and laughter, they craft the divine,
Each tick is a chuckle, each tock is a line.
Crafting eternity with joy and with flair,
In a world where time is both art and a dare.

So let's raise a toast to the whimsical crew,
Who mold time with giggles, turning gray skies to blue.
In the heart of their shop, magic unfolds,
Where laughter is timeless, and the muse never grows old.

Wind-Up Dreams

In a shop of springs and gears,
Wound up folks spin like old piers.
Tick tock chatter fills the air,
Clocks may dance, but they don't care.

A tiny man with pointy shoes,
Winds his thoughts like a Sunday snooze.
He tells his tales with a quirky grin,
While the cuckoo birds just roll on in.

The rivets sing as they jiggle tight,
Bobbing around in the pale moonlight.
Stealing time like a mischievous kid,
With every tick, there's laughter hid.

So, let your worries bloom and grow,
For every turn is a chance to show.
In winding dreams where time does tease,
Just enjoy the ride with utmost ease.

The Art of Precision

In a world of precise tick-tock,
Lives a master at his workshop dock.
With tiny tools and a gentle touch,
He makes each cog work, oh-so-much!

His eyebrows furrow, his tongue in cheek,
Painting numbers, oh so unique.
A clock that sings, a watch that twirls,
Filling the air with ticklish swirls.

He measures with a comical flair,
As springs jump high, spilling everywhere.
"Oops!" he chuckles, "Not quite the plan!"
But laughter is the best of the clan.

With every tick, he slyly grins,
As time ticks forward; it's all in spins.
Creating clocks with a wink and jest,
Where punctuality is surely blessed.

Beneath the Face of Time

Beneath the face of that old clock,
Time plays hopscotch, a silly mock.
Hands reach out like kids at play,
Chasing seconds that run away.

With ticklish tocks, they jump and leap,
A commotion that makes silence weep.
Underneath the gears and grinds,
Are sighs of joy that fate unwinds.

Ticking moments, they pirouette,
While time winks back in a quaint duet.
"Hold on tight! We've miles to go!"
But the jesters just laugh, putting on a show.

So laugh with time, don't take it seriously,
For every tick's a chance to be merry.
Dance with seconds, embrace the rhyme,
Sit back and watch beneath the face of time.

Chronicles of the Hourglass

In an hourglass where grains do swirl,
Lives a funny sprite with a twirl.
He flips the glass, and down they pour,
Silly stories drip to the floor.

Grains reminisce of days gone by,
Whispers of laughter as they fly.
Each tick and tock tells a tale,
Of sandwich fights and epic fail.

Stuck inside, the silly sand,
Makes castles that grow out of hand.
With a giggle and a wink so sly,
It wishes time would just fly high.

So cherish the glass, it's worth the fun,
Every grain, every laugh, when the day is done.
For in the chronicles, time's a friend,
Grains of joy that never end.

Time's Ticking Compass

In a shop where clocks all dance,
A tick-tock tune gives time a chance.
Each face winks with a silly grin,
Time laughs as it begins to spin.

A squirrel stole a golden gear,
For breakfast, it just couldn't veer.
With nuts in paws, it lost the race,
A tangle of wires caused a chase.

The pendulum swings, back and forth,
Telling jokes of time's great worth.
The hands do cha-cha in delight,
As seconds hop away from night.

It's tick-tock chaos, what a sight!
In the clock shop, all feels right.
Each laugh echoes, with every chime,
As we dance along with time.

Gears of Destiny

In a realm where gears collide,
A rusty clock began to slide.
It tripped on oil, made quite a mess,
And laughed aloud in its fine dress.

A feather fell and caused a stir,
The clock whirred loud, made all hearts purr.
With every turn, a giggle soared,
As cogs began to play aboard.

A tiny mouse stole a shiny wheel,
Wore it like a crown, oh what a deal!
With each squeak, the tickers grinned,
For time's wild fun had just begun.

Round and round, the laughter grew,
As gears became a merry crew.
With every tick, a joke resounds,
In this clockwork world, joy abounds.

Precision in Motion

In a workshop filled with whirring sights,
The clock hands spin like silly kites.
With every tick, a dance ensues,
As time dresses in colorful shoes.

A cat named Tickles stole the show,
Chasing shadows, moving to and fro.
With paws on knobs, it gave a twist,
Creating chaos, how could we resist?

The clocks giggled and chimed in glee,
As every second became a spree.
With winks and nods, time's clownish face,
Explores new worlds at a frantic pace.

So let's join in this whimsical race,
Where moments bounce like a merry chase.
With each tick, let joy be the potion,
In this wild dance of precision in motion.

Crafting Minutes

With tiny tools and crafty hands,
Minutes crafted like musical bands.
Screwdrivers dance, like partners do,
As laughter echoes between the two.

One minute slipped and took a stroll,
Tried to sneak back, but lost its goal.
The clock grinned wide, said, 'What a game!'
As every second tried to reclaim.

A butterfly, with wings so bright,
Whispered secrets to the moonlight.
It danced around with giddy cheer,
In a ballet of time, without any fear.

So come and join this joyful spree,
Where minutes laugh and giggle with glee.
Crafting time with a pinch of fun,
In this merry shop, we're never done!

Mastering Minutes

In a shop of springs and gears,
A clock laughed, said, "No fears!"
It ticked and tocked with glee,
"Time's a game, come play with me!"

Old timers, they loved to bicker,
"I'm on time!"
"No, you're quicker!"
Yet, in harmony they prance,
Each to its own little dance.

A pendulum swings, what a sight,
Dropping jokes, left and right.
With every swing, a punchline lands,
A tickled crowd, they clap their hands!

So if you see a clock that's grinning,
Know it's just the time that's spinning.
Join the laughter, don't look shy,
For minutes fly, oh my, oh my!

Chasing Fleeting Seconds

Two seconds ran across the street,
Played hopscotch on my feet.
"Catch us if you can!" they yelled,
As I tripped, then fell, then yelled!

A minute hovered, all too smug,
Sipped coffee, gave a shrug.
"Please don't rush this perfect blend,
Time's a friend, not just a trend!"

A clock that danced, oh what a sight,
Did the cha-cha, left and right.
Seconds laughed and struck a pose,
While a cuckoo laughed, "Here it goes!"

So if you see time chase away,
Join the fun, and let it play.
In this race of joy and cheer,
Fleeting seconds bring us near!

Metronomic Dreams

In a world where dreams tick-tock,
A jester danced atop a clock.
"To the beat of time, we'll sway,"
He winked and shimmied all the way.

Metronomes lined up in a row,
Each one claimed, "I steal the show!"
They clicked and clacked with such delight,
Joking, "We work day and night!"

A dreamer laughed, lost in the sway,
"Can we leap and play all day?"
The metronomes replied with style,
"Come join us, just stay awhile!"

So let's march to this funny beat,
With every moment, feel the heat.
In metronomic dreams we sing,
Life's a song that joy can bring!

The Weight of Time

A scale of time, so heavy, so grand,
Weighed the hours with a gentle hand.
"I'm full of moments," it did say,
"But I prefer to float and play!"

Each hour grumbled, "Don't be bold!"
While laughing seconds broke the mold.
"We're lighter than a feather's float,
Join our race on this little boat!"

A tick-tock turned into a jig,
As the weight of time began to dig.
Minutes chuckled, danced in line,
Said, "Why not make this hour divine?"

So if you find time weighs you down,
Join the jesters in this town.
For laughter makes the burdens light,
In this merry, timeless flight!

Tinkering with Fate

In a shop filled with gears and springs,
He laughs at the chaos time brings.
With a twiddle and a twist of a screw,
He makes seconds dance, then rush like a zoo.

A watch with no hands? Just a clever prank!
He chuckles while clocks pile in a crank.
'Why worry about your schedule,' he beams,
'When I can make time play tricks with your dreams?'

His creations tick-tock in clumsy delight,
The hands move like drunks on a wild night.
As hours bumble forth like playful kids,
He simply grins at what fate always hid.

With a wink he secures the last tiny latch,
Puts a whoopee cushion under a scratch.
Then off he goes, leaving clocks in a whirl,
A master of time, oh what a silly world!

Chronicles of the Time Artisan

In a realm where moments are all but a joke,
A time artisan crafts with a chuckle and poke.
He bound time in a book, full of whimsy and cheer,
Each page tick-tocked loud, like laughter you hear.

Once a minute fell straight from its place,
Rolling around, wearing a comical face.
'You won't get lost!' he said with a shout,
'Just remember where you dropped — it's always about.'

His workshop was wild, clocks everywhere spun,
Each tick a mishap, each tock a pun.
He'd take back the days that went awry,
Fix them with laughter, watch time fly high.

As he fumbles through springs with a grin on his face,
Time chuckles back, keeping up with the race.
In this grand saga of seconds gone by,
Who knew that the past could be so spry?

Harmonizing Minutes

In a symphony of ticks, he finds his delight,
Minutes harmonize in a comical fight.
'You're flat!' yells the hour, 'You can't keep the beat!'
The seconds just giggle, their rhythm's a treat.

He tunes up the clocks with a wrench and a smile,
Strumming the gears in a whimsical style.
'Now play it crescendo — a dance for us all!'
The pendulums sway, and the alarms start to call.

With a wink and a nudge, he conducts the show,
Time's melody bursts, filled with laughter aglow.
A cacophony erupts, but all are in tune,
As seconds leap forth, chasing a balloon.

Oh, what a concert, a slapstick reprise,
Clocks prance onstage, with glittering eyes.
The minutes, once painful, now savor the jest,
Harmonizing time has surely been a quest!

The Dance of Pendulums

Atop the shelf, pendulums swing with glee,
Their dance a spectacle for all eyes to see.
'Watch your toes!' cries a clock, with a wink and a laugh,
As a pendulum twirls, invoking the craft.

Tickle me, time! they joyfully sway,
In jigs and in jives, through night and through day.
Each swing a comment on the folly of haste,
Every chime a reminder of moments misplaced.

Round and around they spin like old fools,
Creating a rhythm that breaks all the rules.
With laughter they whirl in a grand old parade,
A comedy troupe where no joke is afraid.

So here in this space of jolly old clocks,
Time's playful dance puts us all in a box.
The pendulums part as the audience stays,
What a funny show, in a time-warped haze!

A Clockmaker's Legacy

In a dusty shop, gears spin and whir,
A tiny man giggles as he polishes her.
He winds up the past with a laugh and a grin,
Every tick tells a tale of where he's been.

With springs in his pockets, and laughter in tow,
He dances with clocks, moving fast, moving slow.
Each minute a jest, each hour a play,
In a world where time simply runs away.

When clocks start to chime like a chorus of crows,
He claims it's just music that nobody knows.
With a wink and a nod, he adjusts each twist,
Saying "Time isn't serious, how could it be missed?"

As gears spin together in playful delight,
He laughs at the sun for not staying up tight.
With every loud tick, the world turns around,
In this clockmaker's shop, joy just abounds.

Beyond the Face of Time

In a land of clocks, where seconds hang loose,
Ticking away, with a spring in their moose.
A pancake flips high, then lands with a thud,
"Guess time really flies, like a grinning old bud!"

The pendulum dances, a waltz rather weird,
Each swing is a story, slightly appeared.
With laughter like syrup and gears made of cheer,
Time shakes his fist at the clock—"Oh dear!"

With cuckoo birds laughing, then popping outside,
The old clockmaker giggles, he takes great pride.
"Let chaos unfold in every tick-tock,"
As the watches all jump, like a gathering flock.

So cheers for the hours that slip through our hands,
Let's celebrate time with its goofy demands.
For while we may count, let's not take a side,
In the timekeeper's realm where the fun has not died.

Blueprints of Memory

Lost in the sketches of time's swirling art,
He scribbles with laughter, a tick-tocking heart.
Each drawing a joke, each design a pun,
His blueprints of memory, full of rapture and fun.

His tools are marbles and old roller skates,
Every roll of the die shows time's quirky fates.
He calculates laughter with gears made of light,
While clocks shake their heads, "This is purely a sight!"

In the attic of time, the mischief is grand,
With hourglass dancers and a thin rubber band.
He chuckles and whispers, "Just flip it around,"
As memories giggle, time's joy knows no bounds.

So here's to the blueprints, both silly and wise,
Crafted by whimsy, beneath laughing skies.
When time's hands are spinning, and the past's full of cheer,
Memories are giggling, "Oh, we're still here!"

Shadows of Lost Hours

In shadows that wiggle, where lost hours roam,
A clockmaker stumbles, he's far from his home.
With shadows as friends on a whimsical spree,
They plot out a dance that's delightfully free.

The wisps of the past sneak behind every tick,
Joking about sundials, they play their own trick.
"Why hurry," they say, "when we can just play?"
The clockmaker chuckles, "Let the shadows sway!"

With each passing minute, they throw pranks and gags,
Like slipping on seconds and finding lost rags.
They tap dance through time on a soft, silent beat,
In a world where lost hours just can't be beat.

So raise a glass high to the laughter and jest,
For time is a friend, when it's dressed in its best.
Let shadows remind us, as they whirl all night,
That lost hours can play, and still feel just right.

A Symphony of Cogs

In a shop where clocks do dance,
Cogs spin wildly, what a chance!
Tick-tock laughter fills the air,
As springs and gears play without care.

A pendulum winks, a cheeky tease,
Saying, "Hurry up, if you please!"
Each tock a giggle, each tick a jest,
Who knew timekeepers could be the best?

A cuckoo bursts with comic flair,
"I've got no time for your despair!"
A merry band of ticking cheer,
Makes every second worth a year.

In this workshop, joy's the key,
Watchmaking's more than just a spree!
With cogs and laughter, what a sight,
As time ticks on, it feels just right.

Past and Present Entwined

In a world where time gets stuck,
Old clocks chime, "What the duck?"
With gears that grumble, springs that squeak,
Each second's prank is quite unique.

The future's bright and wobbly too,
Laser beams and gadgets blue!
Yet Grandpa's clock still swings and sways,
Making faces in a timeless haze.

We shuffle through the ticks and tocks,
Cracking jokes with rusty locks.
A watch once lost, now found with glee,
Tells tales of time, it's pure comedy!

So raise your glass to past and now,
In tangled time, we take a bow.
With laughter echoing in each chime,
Let's celebrate this silly rhyme.

The Art of Time

Tick-tock, the art on display,
With every click, there's fun at play.
Crafting moments, what a feat,
Making seconds dance to a beat.

A clock with legs? Now that's absurd!
It shuffles about, and it's quite furry!
For every ding, a chuckle rings,
In the clockshop, joy's what life brings.

Springs unwound, they coil and twirl,
Like jesters in a joyful whirl.
Each laughter echoing through the halls,
As clockhands trip and tumble, how it sprawls!

Time isn't serious, oh no not here,
It's a carnival of ticklish cheer!
So let the minutes frolic and chime,
In this merry dance of whimsical time.

Echoes of Ancient Clocks

In the shadows, old clocks grin,
Their whispers tickle, where to begin?
With echoes of laughter from times of yore,
Each chime a joke, we can't ignore.

A grandfather clock with a mustache so grand,
Tells tales of time from across the land.
With every tock, it gives a wink,
Causing listeners to stop and think.

A sundial frowns at sunsets shy,
"Why do I wait? I want to fly!"
In the realm of hours, fun never stops,
With gags and giggles from ancient clocks.

So gather 'round these laughing tales,
Where every tick is laced with gales.
In the echoes of time, we find our place,
Filled with humor, joy, and space.

Navigating Temporal Seas

In a boat made of springs, they sail with glee,
Tick-tock tides carry them, wild and free.
They steer with a pin, and laugh with delight,
As clocks wave their hands in a merry fight.

A whale made of gears swims by with a grin,
Saying, 'Join my dance, it's a clockwork spin!'
The stars are all watches, twinkling so bright,
Guiding the ship through the playful night.

Time flies like confetti, a joyous parade,
As intervals waltz, and hours cascade.
They catch a lost minute in laughter so sweet,
Unraveling moments with whimsical feet.

Sailing through laughter, where moments collide,
The humor of timing, they cannot hide.
With each silly tick, they loop all around,
Navigating the waves of a funny sound.

Cogs and Dreams

In a world full of cogs, where dreams take their flight,
One invented a dragon that ticked through the night.
With a wink and a nod, it danced on the floor,
Spinning tales of clocks that opened the door.

The cogs whispered secrets of laughter and fun,
As wizards in tophats enchanted a pun.
They brewed potions of time in a teapot so grand,
Sipping on giggles while plotting their plan.

Oh, the dreams that they weaved with each turn of a crank,
Dancing around while avoiding the plank.
The clock tower giggled, its hands all askew,
As they spun in a circle, the room quickly grew.

In a realm where the silly and serious blend,
They found joy in cogs, a timeless friend.
With blueprints of laughter that floated on high,
They crafted a world where no one says bye!

Echoes of Lost Time

In a clock shop of echoes, with pings and with pongs,
Whispers of seconds spun silly songs.
A lost hour quipped, 'I've misplaced my pair!'
While minutes played hopscotch without any care.

A calendar juggled its days with delight,
Counting up giggles till late in the night.
The seconds rolled in like a cheeky parade,
While hours performed tricks, and timers displayed.

They chased a missed deadline, it giggled away,
'You can catch me at noon, but only to play!'
Time saw them laughing and swirled in a dance,
Swaying through echoes, they lost all their chance.

In the shop of confusion, with twists and with chimes,
The sound of lost laughter outlasted the crimes.
They found in the chaos, a ribbon of cheer,
Echoes of humor, forever held dear.

The Symphony of Mechanics

In the noisy workshop, a concert took flight,
Tools clanged together and sparks danced with light.
As gears formed a band, each tick found its tune,
Playing symphonies late 'neath the bright, silver moon.

The hammers were drummers, with wrenches on strings,
Releasing the music of wonderful things.
Saws sawed in rhythm, while bolts spun around,
Creating a melody, joyful and sound.

With whistles and fumbles, the discord rang true,
While sprockets played flutes, a humorous crew.
Cogs did a ballet, in synchrony spun,
While clocks stood and cheered, for the concert was fun.

As the final notes echoed, the encore was loud,
Tools took a bow, deeply thankful and proud.
In the symphony grand, where laughter does bloom,
The mechanics of joy filled the sonic room.

Unraveling Time's Threads

In a shop filled with clicks and chimes,
The watchmaker's lost all his rhymes.
With gears that giggle and springs that sway,
He winds his day in a comical way.

A cuckoo bird joins in the fun,
Singing loudly, 'I've just begun!'
With every tick, the laughter grows,
As time takes a break and mischief flows.

His tools are dancing, oh what a sight,
As screws perform in delight.
The clock's hands do a jig and twirl,
In the watchmaker's world, time's a whirl!

So if your watch should lose its cheer,
Just visit the shop that's filled with gear.
For in this realm where seconds collide,
Time is a joke that won't be denied!

The Artisan's Song

With hammers tapping a catchy beat,
The watchmaker dances, oh so fleet.
His goggles slip down, but not his sound,
As the rhythm of ticking joyfully resounds.

There's a tiny mouse on a silver cog,
Wearing a hat made of a coffee log.
With paws so nimble, he helps around,
Turning time with a merry bound!

The pendulum swings, a laugh in its tone,
As it nudges the chin of a sleepy gnome.
He snores in beats, with a wink and a puff,
'Watch out!' cries the mouse, 'It's getting too rough!'

In this workshop, time's always bright,
Where clocks have faces of pure delight.
The watchmaker sings, and the world hums along,
Crafting memories in a playful song!

Timelines Forged by Craft

In the heart of gears, a laugh does brew,
With each tick-tock, mischief ensues.
The hands of time play peek-a-boo,
In a joyful dance, all bright and new.

The watchmaker's mustache twirls and spins,
As clocks crack jokes, like long-lost friends.
'What time is it?' they tease and smear,
'Why, it's always happy hour here!'

An old watch grumbles, 'I need a break!'
'Just tick it out, for goodness' sake.'
With laughter echoing, the gears unite,
Turning seconds into sheer delight.

So if you find time's acting all queer,
Remember the place where it's all sincere.
For in this circus of hands and dials,
Time's just a jester, serving up smiles!

Crafting Broken Moments

In a cluttered workshop, bits and bobs,
The watchmaker sings, while the gear mob throbs.
With a twist and a turn, he fixes the gloom,
Creating laughter to brighten the room.

An alarm clock sneezes, 'A-choo!' it goes,
Tickling the floor with its funny prose.
While the tools have a party on the workbench,
Giggling at gears that groove and clench.

'Why are you broken?' asks a watch so sly,
'Because time flies by and I cannot comply!'
'Join the fun, don't be so blue,
Let's craft up some joy, just me and you!'

With a wink and a smile, the watchmaker thrives,
With every fix, he brings clocks alive.
So visit his world where time's not a chore,
Just quirky moments and laughter galore!

Time's Silent Architect

In a shop with gears and spring,
A fellow works, oh what a fling!
He talks to clocks, they tick in tune,
While making time bend like a balloon.

A watch once yelled, 'I'm late, oh me!'
He laughed, 'You're just a clock, you see!'
With each new tick, a story spins,
Of time's odd dance and playful grins.

He sneezed on one, it coughed a chime,
'Bless you!' laughed the frozen time.
As hours laughed and minutes played,
This watchmaker's antics never stayed.

So come and watch the madness flow,
As time ticks by, both fast and slow.
In a world of cogs and playful clatter,
He's the one who makes it matter.

Reflections in Brass

In a shop where reflections gleam,
Lies a brass fellow with a quirky dream.
He polished his watches, each one a friend,
Said, 'Together we'll time travel, my trend!'

One watch said, 'I tick like a hare!'
The other grinned, 'I'm late, but I care!'
With numbers dancing on every face,
In the race of time, they found their place.

He made them smile with a shiny glaze,
As each tick echoed in whimsical ways.
'Why rush,' he chuckled, 'time is a prank!'
While clocks winked back in their mirrored rank.

So if you hear laughter from a clock,
It's a hint that time's tick-tock is a mock.
In this brass world where echoes cheer,
Through laughter, the minutes disappear.

In Pursuit of Lost Time

He chased lost hours down the street,
Stumbling over shoes and sticky feet.
What a sight, with arms outstretched,
'Come back, you sneaky little wretch!'

As moments giggled and minutes ran,
He tripped on time like a silly man.
'You can't outrun me!' he called with glee,
But tick-tock laughter filled the spree.

With a net made of dreams and feathery grace,
He caught a second, gave it a chase.
But seconds flew, bursting with laughs,
'Why chase us all? Just enjoy the halves!'

So he danced in delight, forgot the main race,
While time spun around in a giggling space.
In pursuit he found, what was truly sublime,
Was living each moment, not just keeping time.

The Keeper's Diary

With quill in hand and a grin on his face,
He scribbles tales of time in a race.
The clocks are characters in his play,
Chasing moments, oh what a fray!

One tick said, 'I'm a race car, you know!'
While another replied, 'I just like to go slow.'
He documented each witty plight,
Of hours getting tangled each silly night.

His diary filled with tales and more,
Of clocks who bounced like kids in a store.
Throughout the pages, laughter fills the air,
In a world where time dances without a care.

So if you see a clock wink at you,
It's signaling it's up for a brew.
In the keeper's tales, time's never a bore,
Just playful mischief, forever in store.

Echoes of Moments Past

In the attic, dusty clocks tick,
Each one telling tales, oh so slick.
A pocket watch sneezes, what a prank,
While an old cuckoo gives me a wank.

Tangled gears, a battle in jest,
Time's little quirks, a comic fest.
I fix the hands, they dance and spin,
As laughter echoes, let the fun begin.

A sundial grins under the sun,
Counting shadows, oh what fun!
In the corner, a calendar sighs,
Every square holds a thousand lies.

Old hourglass, full of sand,
Belly laughs at the time we planned.
In this realm, where time can play,
Moments past are jokes, come what may.

The Keeper of Timeless Tales

A quirky man with a pocket full of springs,
Juggles moments like they're silly things.
Tales of time, he shares with a grin,
Each tick a giggle, where do I begin?

His watch whines like a playful cat,
Says it's tired of the same old chat.
On the wall, a calendar winks,
Time's a comedy, or so it thinks.

With funny gears that shimmy and shake,
He tells of the days that vanish and break.
Like a magic show, he pulls a prank,
The minutes jump, oh, what a clank!

Through whimsical paths where seconds beam,
He carries laughter on the finest seam.
In the world where time can tease,
Moments forgotten, but never with ease.

Unraveling the Fabric of Hours

A spool of time, all tangled and bright,
Threads of laughter woven tight.
He stitches moments, with needle and glee,
Creating a quilt of absurdity.

With every tick, a snicker erupts,
Each loop and twist, a joke interrupts.
A fabric soft, with patches of jest,
A masterpiece made with giggles, not rest.

Old hands spinning yarn, spinning rhyme,
A tapestry painted in foolish time.
He knits the day into sweaters of fun,
While a misfit clock says, 'I'm not done!'

Just as seconds leap, and laughter flows,
The fabric of hours only he knows.
With every stitch, the past has a laugh,
In his playful world, time's just a gaffe.

Time's Unseen Threads

In a workshop filled with whimsical flair,
Threads of time dance in the air.
A needle of laughter, a thread of glee,
Stitching seconds into comedy.

The tick-tock tunes, a musical spree,
Gears giggle softly, just wait and see.
A misplaced minute leads to a fumble,
A timeless laugh, oh what a jumble!

With every moment, he threads a delight,
In the heart of time where chaos takes flight.
It's a network of chuckles, a fabric so bright,
Where every second sparks joy, pure and light.

So join the dance, let whimsy unwind,
In the web of hours, fun's intertwined.
For time is a joke, and oh, what a jest,
In the keeper's realm, we all are blessed.

The Rhythm of Ticktock

In a shop where gears align,
A clock made coffee, just sublime.
It buzzed and ticked with all its might,
Then brewed a cup to my delight.

With every tick, a joke was made,
A pendulum danced in grand parade.
The cogs would laugh, the springs would sing,
A raucous party for everything!

A squirrel came to steal a nut,
Got trapped inside a shiny cut.
Now every hour, he makes a sound,
A riddle where lost things are found!

So here we toast to silly clocks,
Who wear their humor like old socks.
With gears so silly, smiles abound,
In this ticktock laughter's found.

Secrets of the Timekeeper

Behind the brass is quite the tale,
A ticklish secret, nary a fail.
The hour hand winks, the minute grins,
Stealing moments where laughter begins!

The pendulum swings with silly glee,
Telling time with a cup of tea.
Every tick reveals a joke or two,
The timekeeper's secrets, just for you!

A watch with feet? Oh, what a sight!
It jogs around to keep things right.
While the cuckoo sings out, "What's the time?"
With every quip, it sounds like rhyme!

So raise your glass to gears that fumble,
In this world where moments tumble.
With laughter echoing through the space,
Our timekeeper wears a cheerful face.

Beneath the Clock Face

Beneath the clock, I found a maze,
Where gears and springs danced in a blaze.
They tripped on numbers, fell with glee,
A goofy time, just wait and see!

The second hand slipped on a line,
Declared it "slippery!" at half past nine.
A tick-tock tumble, a somersault,
With every round, they'd hear a brawl!

Cogs played tag, wheels spun around,
A funny ruckus, joy unbound.
The clock said, "Time's up!" with a shout,
But giggles lingered, laughed throughout!

So peek beneath, where time takes flight,
In this clock's world, it's pure delight.
With every chime, a joke we hear,
In this grand time, let's all draw near!

Threads of Eternity

In a loom where moments thread,
Time's fabric weaves, a tale widespread.
With every stitch, a giggle tight,
Woven patterns, oh what a sight!

The weaver grinned, forgot his lunch,
"Who needs a meal when time can crunch?"
A tapestry of chuckles grew,
Each loop a laugh, just for you!

With colorful threads, the hours spun,
Every tick a joke, and so much fun.
Through all the laughter and playful cheer,
Time stays bright, forever dear!

So here we find, in every seam,
Threads of eternity weave a dream.
Where silly moments blend and cheer,
In this fabric of fun, we hold it dear.

A Tapestry of Tick and Tock

In a workshop filled with gears,
Laughter rings among the peers.
Clocks with faces, big and round,
Giggles echoing all around.

A sneaky spring leaps out to play,
Tickling hands in a funny way.
Time, it seems, has quite the jest,
Even watches need a rest.

Sundials complain of getting old,
While cuckoo birds start to scold.
With every tick, a joke is spun,
Who knew time could be such fun?

So here's to crafts, both strange and bright,
In the world of time, we find delight.
With every chime, let laughter flow,
In the tick-tock dance, enjoy the show!

Time's Meticulous Weave

In a shop where time stands still,
Threads of seconds weave their thrill.
A needle dances, twirls with glee,
Sewing moments, one, two, three!

Strands of minutes all in knots,
Joking clocks with quirky spots.
With every stitch, a snicker grows,
What's next, a clock that wears a nose?

Petite hands play hide and seek,
Tickling time, oh, isn't it sleek?
A funny fable told by gears,
Time's tight fabric hides its tears.

So as the loom of laughter spins,
Chasing hours that wear silly grins.
In this weave of joy and clock,
A tapestry of tick and tock!

The Journey of Tiny Hands

Tiny hands with curious eyes,
Hitch a ride where laughter lies.
They turn the dials and push the keys,
Inventing giggles with the breeze.

A little wrench starts to prance,
Timepieces join in a silly dance.
Screws pop off, then roll away,
"Catch me if you can!" they say.

Gears whisper jokes in secret tones,
Ticklish springs set silly moans.
With every twist, the hours gleam,
Tiny hands craft quite a team!

In this journey through the clock,
Time plays tricks, it loves to mock.
With humor high, we stand and cheer,
As clocks giggle, we persevere!

An Ode to Mechanisms

Oh, gears and springs, a lively bunch,
With whirs and clicks, they love to munch.
They share the tales of time gone by,
In a language that makes us sigh.

A funny little pendulum swings,
Singing softly of silly things.
With every tick, new jokes align,
From cogs to chains, all laugh in time.

A watch that winks, a clock that grins,
With dials that dance, the fun begins.
Delightful noises fill the air,
Mechanisms jest without a care.

So here's to clocks that tick with cheer,
Making time a joy, my dear!
In this ode to humor and gears,
We celebrate with laughs and cheers!

Ticking Harmony

In a shop filled with gears and springs,
A cat danced to the clock's wild rings.
Tick-tock went his little paws,
Chasing time without a pause.

With each tick, the ladybug cheered,
Joined in by a squirrel, quite weird!
They twirled around the cuckoo's call,
In a carnival, they had a ball.

But then a watch fell, oh so loud,
The critters scattered, all so proud.
Dancing stopped, they feared the clang,
Yet laughter sparked, and joy still sang.

So if you hear that ticking beat,
Just know the fun is hard to cheat.
In this clock shop, time plays a part,
Bringing joy and laughter, that's the art.

The Clockwork Path

Down the road of gears and chimes,
Funny folks play silly rhymes.
A clock ran fast, a watch moved slow,
They argued 'bout who won the show.

A parrot perched upon a clock,
Squawking jokes 'bout every tick-tock.
The more he talked, the more they laughed,
Tickling time, they'd had their craft.

A turtle tried to race a hare,
But lost the plot, just stood and stared.
The hare was late, it seemed in jest,
For time is silly, at its best!

So dance along the path you'll find,
That time is playful, not unkind.
With each tick, a chuckle near,
Life's a clock, so full of cheer.

Whispers of Time

Amidst the cogs, a secret hum,
A monkey plays with a chewing gum.
Bouncing balls in rhythm shine,
He claims he's found a new design!

"Oh dear," says an old, wise clock,
"Don't mess around my little flock!"
But giggles echo through metal halls,
As laughter's light breaks through the walls.

A dragonfly tried on a top hat,
Looked in the mirror, said, "What's that?"
With every twist and turn and grin,
Time's a game we all can win.

So listen closely, hear the rhyme,
In every tick, there's space for time.
Whispers linger in the air,
Reminding us that fun is rare.

Hands of Fate

There once were hands who fought for fun,
Debating seriously, "Who is the one?"
A glove said, "I can hold a drink!"
But the wrist chimed in, "Let's not overthink!"

With each movement, they'd twist and turn,
Creating chaos, oh how they'd yearn!
For every joke and pun they made,
Life ticked on, but never swayed.

They pointed here, they pointed there,
Fate laughed as they lost all care.
With every second, more delight,
Hands of fate danced through the night.

So if you see those hands at play,
Join the fun, don't shy away.
In the clock of life, let laughter soar,
For time is precious, forevermore.

Through the Lens of Time

In a shop with gears and springs,
He chuckled at all the silly things.
A broken watch with a missing hand,
Claimed it couldn't make the next grand stand.

With each tick, he heard a joke,
The clock's face grinned, but then it broke.
He fixed it up with some duct tape,
And sent it out to find its shape.

Time laughed along with every tick,
The hands danced round, all quick and slick.
A pocket watch, dressed in a bow,
Winked at him, and off it would go.

As mornings came with a sunrise bend,
Each clock dialed in a different trend.
He whispered back to every chime,
"You're just another clock to my punchline!"

Time's Hidden Pathways

Down winding roads of ticking bliss,
He wandered dreams, oh what a miss!
A cuckoo bird with a teasing grin,
Sang out tunes to the ticking din.

He strolled past clocks that couldn't chime,
One told jokes, another rapped in rhyme.
A sundial winked as shadows played,
"Don't be late!" it mockingly brayed.

In a corridor of watchful glares,
He met a clock who claimed to wear cares.
"Why the fuss?" he asked with cheer,
"I'm just here for the fun, my dear!"

With gears that giggled and springs that laughed,
He found a clock that gave a craft.
Time danced along, a silly prank,
As laughter echoed from every tank!

Tickling the Hours

With a toolkit bright and plenty of jest,
The watchmaker knew how to tickle best.
At noon, he'd dance, at night, he'd sway,
While clocks would chortle, "What a day!"

A grandpa clock with a long beard of gold,
Told tales of time in a voice so bold.
"Oh dear boy," it wheezed with a grin,
"Tickle my gears, and let the fun begin!"

He zipped and zoomed, pursuing each chime,
Engaged with laughter, lost in time.
A pocket watch snorted, 'What a show!'
As hourglasses rolled in the flow.

With each tickle, the minutes would smile,
In harmony with laughter, all the while.
Joy would burst like confetti in air,
In the ticking world, there's always a flare!

The Poetry of Precision

In a realm where time does tap-dance,
Clocks recited poetry, oh what a chance!
An hourglass hummed a gentle tune,
While the cuckoo laughed, "I'll be back soon!"

His tools were sharp, and wit even sharper,
Adjusting gears made him a heart-stopper.
"Tick tock," he teased, "my hours are rife,
With giggles and snorts, they come to life!"

Every spring had a story to tell,
Of moments that snickered and times that fell.
A pendulum swayed with a playful dance,
Saying, "Come join in, let's take a chance!"

So he spun in a whirl of chaotic delight,
As clocks laughed together, what a sight!
For in this world, ticks were so precise,
In every moment, joy is the spice!

In the Workshop of Hours

In a room where gears align,
The clock ticks out a funny line.
A squirrel steals a prized old watch,
Laughing loudly at the notch.

With springs that bounce and wheels that squeak,
The watchmaker solves a ticklish tweak.
His cat, a master of disguise,
Prowls for prey, with half-closed eyes.

A parrot shouts, 'It's half past snack!'
The wrench slips from his expert knack.
With oil spilled and tools astray,
It's time to laugh and give up play.

At last, the clocks all chime with glee,
Ticking tales of pure esprit.
In a world where chaos reigns,
Each timepiece plays its own refrains.

Rhythm of Eternity

The pendulum swings with grace and charm,
Tickling time without alarm.
Each tock's a giggle, each tick's a tease,
A rhythm that dances with perfect ease.

In the shop, a jester's hat,
Sits atop the old cat.
With every wind, the gears do spin,
A hilarious race, let the fun begin!

Can a clock get tired of its job?
With each new hour, it starts to sob.
But wait! It's just a silly prank,
Playing jokes from its time-tank.

With every chime, a joke unfurls,
As laughter binds the spinning whirls.
Time winks as it passes by,
In this rhythm where giggles fly.

A Tapestry of Timepieces

In a shop of clocks, it's quite a sight,
Where watches dance, oh what a fright!
A fabric woven of tick and tock,
Each thread a laugh on the old clock rock.

A cuckoo sings its own decree,
'I'm late for lunch!' Oh, silly me!
While hourglasses spill jokes on the floor,
Time's crescendo leaves us wanting more.

Sundials frown with jealousy,
As digital mocks with glee.
Yet in this chaos, all in jest,
Each timepiece knows it's for the best.

They tickle time with a wink and smile,
Creating memories that last a while.
In this workshop, laughter reigns,
A tapestry of joy that entertains.

The Timekeeper's Odyssey

A timekeeper set sail on a boat,
With clocks that wobble and almost float.
Each tick a splash, each tock a wave,
In this funny world, all are brave.

His compass? A vintage pocket watch,
That giggles when it finds a botch.
Maps drawn with hours of silliness,
Lead to treasures of sheer bliss.

Amidst the laughs, he sails through time,
With every second, a punchline rhyme.
The horizon blinks, a cheeky jest,
As laughter echoes from east to west.

In this odyssey, the clocks unite,
Ticking together, a pure delight.
With each new hour, they sing their song,
In a world where right and left feel wrong.

The Artistry of Seconds

In a shop of gears and springs,
He crafts with laughter and little sings.
Time ticks by with a playful tease,
As he chases dust bunnies with such ease.

He tunes the clocks to play a song,
While rubber chickens dance along.
Each tick a giggle, each tock a cheer,
His hands move quick as if held dear.

The sundials wink at the moon's shyness,
As misshaped shadows show their slyness.
With every tick, he tightens the jokes,
While smiling at the silent folks.

Between the cogs, his secrets hide,
Of quirky creatures that abide.
In every watch, a story twirls,
With giggly gears and laughter swirls.

Dancing in Tick-Tock

At the edge of every second,
A strange parade has beckoned.
Ticking to a rhythm so absurd,
The clocks all dance, haven't you heard?

Ballet shoes on the pendulum's sway,
As clock hands do the cha-cha all day.
A waltzing hourglass tips with grace,
While snoozing minutes find their place.

In this carnival, no time is lost,
For laughter's the currency, no matter the cost.
With every tick, a joke's unveiled,
And every tock, a punchline hailed.

Join the merry clockwork frolic,
Where time's twist is rather symbolic.
A big brass band makes the moments shine,
As we all dance the jig through time's design.

The Cogs' Whisper

In a room full of ticking contraptions,
Whispers of cogs ignite their reactions.
They gossip about the clocks and their fate,
With grins, they giggle and waddle at a rate.

A sprocket's dream of a life unbound,
A wish to leap into the great beyond.
But looped in gears, they swirl, they spin,
Stuck in a waltz that never begins.

Little springs with boisterous squeaks,
They plot their escape while the big clocks speak.
But oh, what a ruckus it would make,
If the whole clock shop began to quake!

So they whisper soft, and swish a twirl,
In a secret dance, they give a whirl.
For jesters in metal and brass must abide,
As time rolls on with laughter inside.

Intricacies of Eternity

Ticking away, eternity's scheme,
With a jester's head and a clown's dream.
Each second spins a tale of cheer,
In this whimsical world, time draws near.

A circle of gears plays hopscotch fair,
While minutes cruise with a jaunty flare.
With every tick, a chuckle ignites,
As time weaves mischief into the nights.

Long hours hold a cup of tea,
Spilling laughter and glee, you see.
For in this clockwork, joy is the key,
Each tick-tock promises hilarity.

So let's toast to the clocks that delight,
Sprinkling laughter from morning to night.
For in the labyrinth of seconds so grand,
Funny moments are intricately planned.

Moments Built in Brass

In a shop filled with gears, oh so bright,
A clumsy repairman, what a sight!
He tripped on a spring, fell flat on his face,
Said, "You'll never see this in a watchmaker's race!"

With a wrench in one hand, and glue on the floor,
He paused for a snack, right by the door.
Tick-tock went the clock, as time slipped away,
"Is it lunch or is it time? Let's call it a day!"

When he fixed up a watch, it burst into song,
The gears danced around, oh so strong!
But a faulty design led to quite the mess,
Now it sings at odd times, during dinner no less!

So here's to the moments, built in brass,
Where laughter and chaos often surpass.
In a world filled with clocks, so timely and neat,
Our watchmaker's blunders just can't be beat!

Time's Lyrical Clockwork

With a twist and a turn, the gears softly hum,
A watchmaker's humor, oh so much fun!
He polished a bezel, it slipped from his hand,
And flew like a frisbee, good grief, what a plan!

Ticking away, with a wink in his eye,
He sang to the springs, "Watch me get by!"
The pendulum swayed, it wobbled and danced,
Those pesky old parts just wouldn't give him a chance!

A zany contraption, he dreamt up at night,
It ticked with a giggle, what a silly sight!
But the jokes on him, as it ticked out of sync,
Now it chimes for a coffee break, oh don't you think?

Yet in all his mishaps, one thing is clear,
Laughter and clockwork bring joy and good cheer.
So here's to the hours that crackle and chime,
In the clockmaker's workshop, where silliness shines!

Journey of the Tinkerer

A tinkerer's tale filled with giggles galore,
He built a fine clock that flew out the door!
With gears that spun wildly, it zipped down the street,
Chasing after pigeons, oh, what a feat!

On a quest for perfection, he made quite the scene,
With whistles and chimes, it was rather obscene.
But amidst all the chaos, he stopped for a break,
And poured out some tea, for heaven's sake!

With each little mishap, he laughed like a fool,
His heart was a clock that ticked with no rule.
He danced with the cogs, in a whimsical whirl,
His workshop a circus, where laughter would twirl!

In the journey of tinkering, day after day,
He found that the joy overshadows the gray.
So let gears spin in mischief, let clocks laugh away,
For every wild journey, brings humor our way!

In Mechanical Harmony

In a world of cogs and whirring delight,
A madcap mechanic worked day and night.
With a grin on his face and oil on his shirt,
Each clock he assembled went crazy, not flirt!

One clock had a hiccup, another went pop,
"Heavens!" he chuckled, "Will this ever stop?"
As springs did a tango and pistons would sway,
He danced through the chaos, come what may!

He tuned up a watch, it belched out a tune,
While telling the time with a laugh and a swoon.
"Who needs a schedule? Just follow my lead,
Let laughter and gears be the heart of our creed!"

In mechanical harmony, they spun and they twirled,
Creating a ruckus that gleefully swirled.
For in every tick, and each chirp from a clock,
Lies a humor-filled dance, around the old block!

In the Hands of Precision

In a tiny shop, just a tick,
Gears and springs dance, oh what a trick!
Each little piece, in harmony chime,
Precision's laughter, caught in time.

A slip of a tool, a wrench goes wild,
Watchmaker chuckles, just like a child.
With every mishap, a lesson learned,
For every watch, a twist has turned.

Cogs are spinning, time plays coy,
Mistakes become art, oh what a joy!
Screws that wobble, find their own way,
Tick tock giggles, brighten the day.

With a wink and a smile, he sets forth,
Laughter and gears, what a great mirth!
In his merry shop, nothing's amiss,
Time's funny games, can't resist this!

Whispers of Wound Springs

In dusty corners, springs do sigh,
With whispers of secrets, oh my, oh my!
They twirl and wiggle, in mischief they play,
Time bends and stretches, come what may.

A spring once tangled, in a playful twist,
Spoke to the watch, 'You can't resist!'
Together they giggled, as hours flew by,
While hands went round, with a wink in the eye.

In frantic moments, they dance with glee,
Each tick a chuckle, joyful decree.
"Wound me tight!" one spring did insist,
The watchmaker laughed, "You're hard to resist!"

In every tick-tock, a giggle is seen,
As time pirouettes, sprightly and keen.
From dawn to dusk, joy fills the air,
In the realm of precision, laughter is rare!

Hourglass Reflections

With grains of sand, carefully poured,
An hourglass grins, never bored.
Time's little jester, in a glassy frame,
Each drop of moment plays the game.

As hours slip by, it starts to chuckle,
Saying, "Hey, stop! Your time's in a jungle!"
Old timekeeper, with a wise old wink,
"Don't blink too fast, or you'll miss the link!"

Between the shifts, it dances around,
With clinks and clanks, a joyous sound.
In every grain, a secret is spun,
Turning moments into laughter and fun.

With each little flip, it bows and grins,
Telling tales of where time has been.
A playful reminder, just take a look,
Life's a quirky little storybook!

Crafting Moments

With hands so deft, he crafts each piece,
Moments are fashioned, much like a fleece.
A tick and a tock, like a joyful song,
In the chaos of time, where hearts belong.

With laughter that echoes, he shapes reality,
Playing with seconds, such pure quality.
He glances at clocks, with a grin on his face,
Creating sweet memories, a jubilant chase.

"Where'd that hour go?" the timekeepers tease,
As he juggles with moments, like summer's breeze.
Each tick a story, each tock a laugh,
In the art of making, he finds his craft.

So when you check time, don't fret or stew,
For in every second, there's joy for you.
With clocks full of laughter, he shares what's dear,
Crafting bright moments, year after year.

www.ingramcontent.com/pod-product-compliance
Lightning Source LLC
Chambersburg PA
CBHW062110280426
43661CB00086B/426